Van Ey

GW01401453

J. Cyril M. Weale

Alpha Editions

This edition published in 2024

ISBN : 9789362923035

Design and Setting By
Alpha Editions
www.alphaedis.com
Email - info@alphaedis.com

Contents

PLATE I.—THE ADORATION OF THE LAMB

(By Hubert van Eyck)

The centre-piece of the Ghent Polyptych, in the Cathedral of that town. The panel was completed in or before 1426. See page 28.

John.   Hubert.

I
THE ADVENT OF THE VAN EYCKS

THE advent of the Van Eycks is the most important landmark in the history of painting in northern Europe. With them we open an entirely new chapter, for although the value of oil in various inferior processes of the art had been ascertained and availed of at an earlier period, it was entirely due to their long and painstaking experiments that its use was perfected as the vehicle of colouring matter in picture-painting. Unfortunately, time and its worst incidentals have obliterated the evidence which would have enabled us to follow the development of this new method, just as they have robbed us of all the earlier work of its original expounders, leaving us at the same time much too inconsiderable remains for a comprehensive survey of the school of which they were the finished product. It is a disconcerting experience to encounter primarily the lifework of two such eminent painters at a stage when they were already in the plenitude of their powers, and an experience that must always tax the ingenuity of the student and critic of their art. Particularly is this the case in respect of the elder brother, for the ascertained facts of Hubert's history are restricted to the last two years of his life (1425-26), while of the masterpieces he bequeathed to posterity only one can be said to be absolutely authenticated, though of others generally ascribed to him several may safely be accepted as genuine. John's career, on the other hand, can be traced back to 1424, but the chronology from that date to his death in 1441 is fairly ample, while he has left us a rich heritage of attested paintings to exemplify the varying aspects of his remarkable genius.

PLATE II.—CHOIR OF ANGELS

(By Hubert van Eyck)

The first dexter lateral panel in the upper zone of the interior of the Great Polyptych: now in the Royal Gallery, Berlin. Painted in or before 1426. See page 31.

It was in the nature of things that the monastic institutions, which in the early Middle Ages were exclusively the nurseries of learning and of the arts and crafts, should have infected these with the mystic spirit induced by the more or less contemplative life its inmates led. More especially must this have been so when we consider that their labours were wholly in the service of religion. As time went on, and monasticism progressed from the pursuit to the dissemination of knowledge, the pupils developed under its influence were naturally imbued with the same spirit, and so a tradition grew up and spread which held undisputed sway for a considerable period in the various centres where artists congregated and formed schools. In the earlier Rhenish school of Cöln this was the dominant note of its art, which it cherished and sustained in all its purity and simplicity to a later period than any of its offshoots and rivals; for as its teaching extended, more particularly northwards, we are conscious of a weakening of its traditions, of a gradual evolution from the spiritual idealism of its mystic brotherhood to the more humanistic realism that is the distinctive feature of Netherlandish art, from the utter sinking of personality to the frank assertion of individuality. Nor does this divergence necessarily bespeak a weakening of religious vitality: rather is it to be ascribed to a marked difference of temperament and race characteristics. Neither could this change have been as abrupt as might appear from the scant remains of the art of the period. It was a natural growth, the one inherent quality of all such developments, ever tending to the elaboration of a higher type, and eventually producing its finest exemplification in the person of Hubert van Eyck. In his younger brother, on the other hand, who almost belonged to another generation, we soon note a more striking falling away from the earlier ideals, and in the event an almost total emancipation from the canons of the mystic school, the explanation of which is probably to be sought in an equally marked difference of character and temperament in the two brothers: the one more poetic and imaginative, the other more objective and materialistic; the one drawing his inspiration from a humble and devout cultivation of art by the light of the sanctuary, the other from a devotion to art for art's sole sake, involving all the difference that divides the expression of beauty of thought and mere beauty of form, the spiritual and the intellectual: each nevertheless supreme in his own sphere, and wielding an influence and authority destined to leave their impress on all the after-work of the school.

II
HUBERT'S NOVITIATE

The small rural town of Maaseyck, on the left bank of the Maas, in the old duchy of Limburg, was the home of the Van Eycks and the birthplace of the elect of their stock, Hubert's coming being traditionally associated with the year 1365, John's with 1385. In the absence of documentary evidence to the contrary, these data are acceptable as founded on reasonable conjecture. There is no record of their parentage, but we know of a third brother, named Lambert, and of a kinsman, one Henry van Eyck, whose exact relationship has not been established. As the early instinct of genius revealed the true bent of the elder lad's disposition, the outstanding advantages of a distinguished school of painting within hail almost of their doors naturally appealed to parents anxious to give effect to their son's aspirations; so to Maastricht they turned, where the boy was duly apprenticed to one or other of its recognised masters. Having served his articles and in due course been admitted to the rank of journeyman, the youthful artist, now free to qualify for his mastership, entered upon the most interesting period of his education, a period largely spent, according to the custom of the time, in foreign travel; and it is with this stage of Hubert's career that criticism first finds legitimate occupation.

Futile as would be the attempt to trace a definite itinerary, it is allowable to conjecture that the mother school of Cöln would mark the first stage in the young artist's travels: in the centre-piece of the great polyptych we discover in the background architectural work distinctly reminiscent of that city, and detail unmistakably Rhenish in character, testifying to a close acquaintance with the district. Evidence of similar import, such as the cathedral in the Louvre picture and the city view with a faithful presentation of Old Saint Paul's as seen from the south in that of Baron Gustave Rothschild's collection, on the confident assumption that these are from the brush of Hubert, bespeak visits to France and England; while the landscape work in all his paintings betrays so intimate an acquaintance with central and southern European scenery as almost to compel us into the beaten tracks of the wandering artist-student of the time through Switzerland and the south of France, to sunny Italy and erubescent Spain. The variety of his mountain scenery—undulating hills and snow-capped peaks, rugged crags and Alpine heights; the depth of his liquid skies and spacious firmaments, with their marvellous cloud and light effects, melodies in colour that breathe the warmth of a southern sun; and the extent of his botanical lore, embracing the olive and citron, the stone pine and cypress, the date-palm and palmetto, naturalised exotics of the Mediterranean slopes—all these and other particulars too numerous to list bear the hall-mark of knowledge garnered in the observant pursuit of local colouring.

For so much there is ample warrant, and within the limits of such guarded conclusions the critic incurs little danger from the many pitfalls that beset the by-paths of deductive reasoning. But seeing that the most of our knowledge of Hubert's life-work is arrived at by this method of inquiry, it is essential that every inference should at least stand the test of probability. To argue, for example, from the presentation of a particular palm-tree a pilgrimage to the Holy Land is to offend the laws of proportion; to discern in the picture of the walled city of Jerusalem in "The Three Marys at the Sepulchre" work evidently "from a sketch made on the spot" would appear more justifiable, until one is reminded of the fact that the defences of the Holy City, pulled down in 1239, were not rebuilt until 1542; but surely it is speculation run riot, in the attempt to vindicate a preconceived theory, when the simple, unobtrusive artist is made, "after the adventurous manner of his time," to join a crusade and journey to Palestine, seeing that the last of these gallant enterprises had taken place full seventy years before he ever saw the light of day. Without, however, incurring the reproach of outraging probability, we may apportion the usual four years of Hubert's term of journeymanship between the countries already indicated, his wanderings likely enough terminating with the visit to England before his return to the Low Countries to settle down to his life's work as a master painter, his range of knowledge tremendously enlarged, his technique broadened and perfected in the various schools and workshops through which he had passed, his imagination fertilised, his creative powers strengthened, his faculty of utterance and expression developed—in short, fully equipped at all points to startle the world with the first-fruits of his as yet unrealised genius.

III
THE GREAT POLYPTYCH

So, back to Maaseyck and to Maastricht: to family rejoicings and the generous welcome of old friends, no light matter when ordered on the good old Netherlandish scale. Anxiety there, of course, and much curiosity here, as to how the promise of early talent would be justified by the ripening fruit. Nor could the issue have been long in doubt. The indispensable test triumphantly passed, the customary formalities duly complied with, and Hubert van Eyck took his place among the master painters of his time, soon to claim rank among the élite of them all. Of wife or children not a whisper, but in an age when civism spelt patriotism, and marriage was recognised as one of the prime moral obligations of a loyal citizen, it is inconceivable that a man of his sterling sense of duty should have done other than conform to the established practice. His home and workshop were from the outset probably cheered by the presence of his younger brother John, fired by the born artist's enthusiasm to follow in his senior's footsteps. This Maastricht studio no doubt also witnessed the inception of that long series of experiments, secretly shared in by the two brothers until carried to perfection, which gave to the world the new art of oil-painting, and so laid all the after ages under the deepest obligation to them.

PLATE III.—PORTRAIT OF "TYMOTHEOS"

(By John van Eyck)

A Presentation Portrait, probably from the Painter to his friend "Timothy," a Greek humanist whose Christian name only is known. The inscription at the foot reads: "Actum anno Domini 1432, 10 die Octobris, a Iohanne de Eyck." No. 290 in the National Gallery, London. See pages 63, 64.

John's apprenticeship ended, and he in turn started on his travels, Hubert would appear to have removed to Holland, where painters and miniaturists of the early years of the fifteenth century repeatedly exhibit marked traces of his influence; where also miniatures in a Book of Hours, of date 1412 to 1417, to the order of Count William for the use of his only daughter, the fair and ill-starred Jacqueline, are judged to have been executed by him on the strength of the many points of resemblance they bear to the Great Polyptych. The commission of the latter work itself is now confidently attributed to the same prince. Observe the prominence given to the tower of Saint Martin's at Utrecht and the adjacent view of Cöln in the centre-piece, "The Adoration of the Lamb," and to St. Martin himself, the patron saint of

Utrecht, in the panel of "The Knights of Christ," the banner in his grasp, moreover, charged with the arms of that town: the Count's territory was in the diocese of Utrecht and the ecclesiastical province of Cöln. So much depends on the origin of this commission in apportioning the respective share each of the brothers had in its execution that the further fact must not be overlooked that Ghent, for which the great work was completed, had no sort of connection with either Utrecht or Cöln, being in the diocese of Tournay and the ecclesiastical province of Rheims, while the only saint in the altar-piece specially connected with Ghent who is characterised by an emblem—St. Livin, to wit—was also widely venerated in Zeeland. Finally, not to labour this aspect of the question unduly, the inscription on the frame attributes, not the picture's inception, but its completion, to Jodoc Vyt, the eventual donor—a form of words so singular as to admit of no other interpretation than the plain meaning the expression conveys.

Count William passed away on the 31st of May 1417, leaving an only child, Jacqueline, aged seventeen, by his wife, Margaret of Burgundy, who had predeceased him. Her uncle, John of Bavaria, Prince-Bishop of Liège, an unscrupulous ruffian who clearly paid small deference to women's rights, at once set himself to rob the unfortunate princess of her possessions. In September 1418 he marched out on Dordrecht, where he established his headquarters; Gorcum and other strongholds speedily succumbed to his arms, and after an interval, during which he married Elizabeth of Görlitz, Duchess of Luxemburg and widow of Anthony of Burgundy, Duke of Brabant and Limburg, he finally removed to Holland and installed himself at The Hague, free now to pursue his nefarious projects. For thirteen years the country resounded with the clash of arms and laboured in the rough and tumble of civil warfare: hence an atmosphere the least congenial to the cultivation and patronage of high art. The cities of Flanders and Brabant were the gainers by the exodus of craftsmen that presently set in. Of their number, sooner or later, was Hubert, who, prior to 1425 at any rate, had already settled at Ghent and acquired the freedom of that city. News of the unfinished polyptych remaining on his hands soon came to the ears of Jodoc Vyt, a wealthy burgher, who eagerly embraced the opportunity of striking the bargain by which he acquired all rights in the picture and so linked his name and personality for all time with this ineffable monument of the painter's art.

In the centre-piece, "The Adoration of the Lamb" (frontispiece), we discover the keynote to the scheme of the work, in the Apocalyptic Vision of St. John the source of its inspiration. The Lamb without spot, the blood from its breast pouring into a chalice, is stood on an altar, the white cloth over which bears on its superfrontal the text from the Vulgate, "Behold the Lamb of God, who taketh away the sins of the world," and on its stole-ends the legend, "Jesus, the Way, the Truth, and the Life." Worshipping angels gather around, some bearing instruments of the Passion, others swinging censers, their smoke laden with the prayers of the saints. In the foreground the Fountain of Life, flowing down through the ages along the gentle slope of flower-bejewelled sward, or dispensing its waters in vivifying jets from the gurgoyles beneath the feet and from the vases in the hands of the winged angel above its standard. To the four quarters groups of the elect: on the near right those of the Old Law and among the Gentiles who had lived in expectation of the Redeemer, the balancing group on the left typical of the New Law—prophets, doctors, philosophers, and princes in the former, the Apostles, popes, bishops, abbots, deacons, monks, and clerics among the latter. The corresponding groups back of the altar represent the army of martyrs whose blood is the seed of the Church, and the multitude of virgins. Over all, from the Holy Dove poised high over the altar, dart rays of light, emblematic of the Wisdom which had inspired their lives and of the fire of Love that had heartened their sacrifice. A carpet of flowers fills in all the open space fore of the altar, flowering shrubs and trees that of the mid-distance, while the entire background is an exquisite example of the realistic landscape-work that is an abiding charm of the Netherlandish school. The wonderful harmony of colour appeals at once to the senses; but more arresting, on nearer acquaintance, for its quality and felicity, is the wide range of portraiture that distinguishes the piece. From the two lateral panels in the dexter shutter the Knights of Christ and the Just Judges are pressing forward to the scene of the Vision, from the corresponding ones in the sinister shutter the Holy Hermits and the Holy Pilgrims: the former on spirited horses—an animal for which the painter evinces a special affection—the latter on foot. These panels are even more remarkable perhaps than the centre-piece for the diversity and multiplicity of the types portrayed, and for the wealth of landscape relieved by bird life lavished in their embellishment.

The "Adoration of the Lamb" is dominated in the upper zone by a triple panel, the centre framing the Almighty enthroned in majesty, whose is the kingdom, the power, and the glory—a supreme conception of the Eternal Father, unequalled for majestic stillness of face, intellectual power of brow, and depth and placidity of vision; on His right is the Mother of Christ, testifying to the full the lowliness of the handmaiden of the Lord, on His left St. John the Baptist, an earnest type, long of hair and rugged of beard, barefooted, and in a raiment of brown camel's hair girdled about the loins, intensifying the austerity of life ordained for him who was to prepare the way of the Lord and make straight His paths. In the "Choir of Angels" (Plate II.), which is the subject of the first lateral panel in the dexter shutter, we have one of the choicest gems of the polyptych, and it affords us a measure of the distance the realistic tendencies of the painter had carried him from the traditions of the mystic school. Justified by the warrant of Scripture, he translates these spirit beings into purely human frames, but with a nerve system attuned to material sensations. In these angels there is no suggestion of trance-like ecstasy in contemplation of the Beatific Vision; they are angels materialised whose features reflect the strain of sustained effort and the underlying sense of pain which in man is inseparable from the sensing of intense joy. Evidently the master had fathomed the secrets of the human heart: the sense possibilities of the spirit world were without his ken, so he humanised his angels and evolved types understandable of the people, and at the same time one of the finest angel groups of all art. So inexpressibly realistic are his conceptions that to the poet-biographer Van Mander, at any rate, it was actually possible to discern "the different key in which the voice of each is pitched." But poets are privileged beings. Accompanying the Choir in their song of praise with organ, harp, and viol are the balancing group of angels in the corresponding compartment of the sinister shutter, types that, strangely enough, are in striking contrast to the former, their features moulded in placid contentment. The extreme panels of this zone are occupied by life-size presentations of our First Parents after the Fall, nude figures painted from the life, with absolute fidelity to nature and masterly conception of type: in a demi-lunette over the figure of Adam we see Cain and Abel making their offerings unto the Lord, and in that over Eve the slaying of Abel at the hands of his brother. There is a tradition extant that the altar-piece was originally furnished with a predella painted in distemper, a picture probably of Limbo or of Purgatory, but no trace of this remains.

PLATE IV.—PORTRAIT OF THE PAINTER'S FATHER-IN-LAW

(By John van Eyck)

The subject of this painting has only within recent months been identified as the father of Margaret van Eyck, with whose portrait, reproduced in Plate VII., it should be compared. The framework bears along the upper border the Painter's simple motto "Als ich can," and at the foot "Iohannes de Eyck me fecit anno 1433, 21 Octobris." No. 222 in the National Gallery, London. See page 66.

The closed shutters display, filling in the full width of the middle zone, the scene of the Annunciation. The Ethyrean Sibyl and the Cumaean Sibyl occupy the demi-lunettes above the middle portion of the Virgin's chamber, the lunettes above the lateral divisions showing half-length figures of the Prophets Zacharias and Micheas. Of the four compartments of the lower zone the inner ones contain statues in grisaille of St. John the Baptist and St. John the Evangelist, the outer ones figures in the attitude of prayer, eminently life-like, of the donor, Jodoc Vyt, and his wife, Elizabeth Borluut. Jodoc was the second son of Sir Nicholas Vyt, Receiver of Flanders,—a wealthy citizen who owned the lordships of Pamele and Leedberghe, besides several mansions in Ghent, of which city he was burgomaster in 1433-34, after filling various minor municipal offices: by no means a handsome type, though manifestly a capable and kindly burgher, well-set, with a somewhat low forehead, small grey eyes, and a large mouth with broad under-lip;

neither do the short-cropped hair and growing baldness or the three warts on upper-lip, nose, and forehead make for attractiveness. In respect of looks his wife is the better favoured, striking the beholder as an indulgent lady, with much of the homely dignity and serenity of the finer type of Flemish matron.

The Great Polyptych had not yet reached completion when, on the 18th of September 1426 Hubert van Eyck passed away after a painful illness. How much of the work remained to be accomplished none can tell with any hope of approach to certainty. A whole volume would not suffice for a critical examination of the mass of contending theories that for the best part of a century has been squandered in the endeavour to allocate to the two brothers their respective shares in the execution of the picture. Remember that it had already been some ten years in the making, and that, although it did not receive its final touches from the brush of John van Eyck until 1432, nearly six years after his brother's death, this period of John's life, as we shall presently discover, was too fully occupied in the service of Duke Philip of Burgundy to have allowed of his spending any considerable proportion of it in the task of completion. Remembering also that John's art had been closely modelled on that of his brother, that none better comprehended his ideals or was more intimately acquainted with the working out of his conceptions, mindful, moreover, of the deep veneration in which he held his master's genius, we must suppose that he realised the obligation of conscientiously adhering to the art and technique of the picture as he found it, any obtruding originality in violation of which would have amounted almost to sacrilege: all this further enhances the difficulty of differentiating between the work of the two painters. Indeed, if so minded, the reader is probably as well equipped as the writer to solve the puzzle.

PLATE V.—JOHN ARNOLFINI AND JOAN CENANI, HIS WIFE

(By John van Eyck)

An incomparable example of the Master's varied gifts, and a valuable study of contemporary dress and domestic furniture. Joan Cenani is presumed to have been a younger sister of Margaret van Eyck, with whose portrait, reproduced in Plate VII., it should be compared. The carved frame of the mirror on the far wall enshrines ten small medallions, exquisite miniatures representing the Agony in the Garden, the Betrayal and St. Peter's Assault on Malchus, Christ led before Pilate, the Scourging at the Pillar, the Carrying of the Cross, Calvary, the Deposition, the Entombment, the Descent into Limbo, and the Resurrection. On the wall above the mirror we read the precise statement, "Iohannes de eyck fuit hic 1434." No. 186 in the National Gallery, London. See page 67.

Hubert van Eyck was laid to rest in the crypt of the chapel for which he had painted his masterpiece, but in 1533, when chapel and crypt had to make way for a new aisle, his remains were transferred to the churchyard, all except the bone of the right fore-arm, which was suspended in an iron casket in the porch of the Cathedral. The brass plate bearing the well-known epitaph was at the same time placed in the transept, only to become the spoil of the Calvinist Iconoclasts in 1578, when already the casket had somehow or other long since disappeared. But what of the painter's fame, to whose workshop laymen of the highest distinction had felt it a privilege to be admitted, about whose easel journeymen painters had flocked, and whom the leading contemporary artists of the Netherlands had been proud to call master? During his lifetime, and for a considerable period after his death, his was a dominating influence in the Art of the North, and Van Mander has it on record that whenever the polyptych was freely exposed to the public gaze crowds flocked to it from morning till night "like flies and bees in summer round a basket of figs and grapes." But in the stress and turmoil of succeeding generations his memory gradually faded away; his work, uncared for, lost hold on the imagination; even his great masterwork narrowly escaped destruction. Even so it did not escape dismemberment, or profanation at the hands of the "restorer." Saved from the fury of the Iconoclasts in 1566, and subsequently rescued from the Calvinist leaders who contemplated its offer to Queen Elizabeth in acknowledgment of her subsidies, it eventually became the spoil of the French Republicans; but after the battle of Waterloo restitution was effected, and the main portion of the altar-piece, all that remains of it in Ghent, was reinstated in its present position. The Adam and Eve panels, which in 1781 had offended the unsuspected modesty of Joseph II., and in consequence been deferentially removed, were ultimately ceded to the Belgian Government, and now rest in the Royal Gallery at Brussels; while the other six shutter panels, which had been safeguarded through the French occupation, were shamelessly sold to a dealer in 1816 by the Vicar-General and churchwardens—in the absence, it is right to say, of the Bishop—for a paltry 3000 florins, subsequently changing hands for 100,000 francs, and eventually becoming the property of the Prussian Government for four times that amount.

IV
IN THE SERVICE OF BURGUNDY

During the five years that followed the death of William IV., Count of Holland and Zeeland, the usurping John of Bavaria had so far succeeded in asserting his power as to be able to permit his interest to wander to the lighter occupations of life, the while the niece he had dispossessed was supplementing the tale of her political woes with all the domestic misery attendant upon a succession of unhappy marriages. Thus in 1422 we find John van Eyck attached to the Count's household as painter and "varlet de chambre," and, as we gather from the prince's household accounts, engaged in the decoration of the palace at The Hague from the 24th of October in that year till the 11th of September 1424. Another member of the household at the time was his kinsman, Henry van Eyck, the record of whose faithful services won him in February 1425 the post of master of the hunt to Jacqueline's second husband, John IV., Duke of Brabant. John of Bavaria died on the 25th of January 1425, and, as might have been expected, civil war immediately broke out. The situation proving uncongenial, the whilom court painter lost no time in taking the road to Flanders, where Philip III., Duke of Burgundy, was lording it as the most munificent patron of the arts and sciences and of letters. With a keen eye for available talent, this princely despot at once enlisted him in his service. No doubt he had become acquainted with the Van Eycks during his residence at Ghent in the days of his heir-apparentship and before the younger artist's removal to The Hague; probably the portrait of Michelle of France, the Duke's first wife (who died in July 1422), copies of which exist, was painted by John: at any rate we have Philip's own words for the fact that it was personal knowledge of John's skill that determined his appointment on the 19th of May 1425 as painter and "varlet de chambre," with "all the honours, privileges, rights, profits, and emoluments" attaching to the office; moreover, with characteristic prudence, he secured a first lien on his services by awarding him a retaining fee—call it salary or call it pension—equivalent to £5, 11s. 1-1/3d. in contemporary English currency, or anything from ten to twelve times that sum at the present day.

Having made good his position, John's first move apparently was in the interest of his kinsman, for whom he secured the position of falconer in the ducal household. As we have no further concern with this member of the Van Eyck family, it may be said that in 1436 he was employed by the Duke on a secret mission of some importance, that on the occasion of his marriage in 1444 to the daughter of the master-falconer Philip made him a present of 100*l.*, and that in 1461 he became baillie of the town and territory of Termonde, continuing in that office, with the additional distinctions of councillor and chamberlain to the Duke, besides a knighthood, until his death in November 1466.

The new court painter was something more than a master of his art: a man evidently of sterling qualities of mind and heart, of wide accomplishments and business capacity—in every way *persona grata* at the most brilliant court of the age. Not many months after his appointment he removed to Lille by order and at the expense of the Duke, by whom also was paid the rent of the house he occupied there from 1426 to 1428, from midsummer to midsummer. Of his professional work at this period nothing is known. The chroniclers in the Duke's service did not concern themselves with such minor matters. As De Comines himself boasted, they wrote "not for the amusement of brutes and people of low degree, but for princes and other persons of quality," little bethinking themselves what store the after ages would have set by their gossip had it busied itself with the doings, for example, of court painters. In other respects, however, we are better served, and in the early part of 1426 we find John van Eyck commissioned, after the pious custom of the time, to undertake a pilgrimage in the interest of the ducal health, and in August of the same year despatched on some distant foreign mission. His return was saddened by tidings of the death of his brother Hubert, who had passed away in his absence. Further tokens of the ducal favour in 1427 took the form of presents of 20*l.* and 100*l.* respectively.

Duke Philip's matrimonial ventures hitherto had not been crowned with success. Neither his first wife, Michelle of France, nor Bonne of Artois, whom he wedded and lost within the ten months (she died in September 1425), had provided him with an heir. Anxious to secure the succession in the direct line, towards the middle of 1427 he despatched ambassadors to the court of Alphonsus V., King of Aragon, to obtain for him the hand of Isabella, eldest daughter of James II., Count of Urgel, and John van Eyck was attached to the mission. Arriving at Barcelona in July, only to find that the earthquakes in Catalonia had driven the Court to escape by sea to Valencia, the embassy followed in the royal track and reached this city early in August, in time for the floral games and bull-fight with which the Jurats honoured the King. The mission led to nothing, not even to a portrait of the princess, who in September 1428 was married to Peter, Duke of Coimbra, third son of John I., King of Portugal; but it is interesting to find Alphonsus V. in later years acquiring paintings by Van Eyck for his collection. The return journey included a short halt at Tournay, where the magistrates very appropriately paid Van Eyck the compliment of a wine of honour on the 18th of October, St. Luke's Day, the local guild, moreover—Robert Campin, Roger de la Pasture, and James Daret doubtless distinguished among its members—being favoured with his company in the celebration of the feast of its patron saint. A like wine of honour was presented to the ambassadors on the 20th.

An illuminating dispute between the Duke, the Receiver of Flanders, and John van Eyck helped to relieve the tedium of life in the intervals of employment on foreign missions at this stage of the painter's career. Philip's munificence was largely tempered by prudent frugality in the ordering of his household, and in the process of curtailing his domestic expenses in 1426 he published an edict bearing date December 14 regulating its constitution and the wages of its members. By some inadvertence John's name was omitted from the new roll, and the Receiver of Flanders summarily stopped payment of his salary. An ineffectual protest was lodged, complaints followed reinforced by threats, to such good purpose that eventually, though not until after many months' persistent badgering, the aggrieved party emerged with flying colours from the triangular duel, securing letters patent under date March 3, 1428, confirming his appointment and commanding the payment of all arrears.

PLATE VI.—THE VIRGIN AND CHILD, ST. DONATIAN AND ST. GEORGE, AND CANON G. VAN DER PAELE

(By John van Eyck)

The largest but one of the Painter's works, unfortunately damaged by cleaning and clumsy retouching, while the general effect is marred by a thick coating of cloudy varnish. The white shame-cloth about the Child's loins is a later addition. At the foot on the original frame we read: "Hoc opus fecit fieri magister Georgius de Pala huius ecclesie canonicus per Iohannem de Eyck pictorem: ... completum anno 1436°." In the Town Gallery, Bruges. See page 74.

Of the many paintings executed by John van Eyck to which no precise date can be attached not one can with certainty be ascribed to this period, and yet it is difficult to believe that his duties in the three years he had already spent in the ducal service were exclusively of a non-professional character: surely the lost portrait of Bonne of Artois as Duchess of Burgundy, a copy of which is preserved in the store-room of the Royal Gallery at Berlin, was his work. The years immediately following, however, yielded a rich harvest of brilliant pictures, first among which, chronologically, two portraits of the Infanta Isabella of Portugal. Philip, on matrimonial projects still intent, was now turning his attention from the Courts of Spain to the neighbouring one of Portugal, and in the autumn of 1428 he decided on an embassy to John I.

The mission was a princely one: at its head Sir John de Lannoy, councillor and first chamberlain; associated with whom were Sir Baldwin de Lannoy, governor of Lille—at some later date, too, a subject for our painter's brush—high dignitaries of the court and some of the leading gentry, a secretary, cupbearer, steward, clerk of accounts, and two pursuivants, and last, but not least, John van Eyck, whose relative standing may be gathered from the fact that in the distribution of gratuities at the ceremony of leave-taking only that of the chief ambassador exceeded his, the respective sums being 200*l.* and 160*l.* The mission, distributed between two Venetian galleys, sailed out of Sluus harbour on the 19th of October and arrived the next day at Sandwich, where three or four weeks were spent awaiting a further escort of two galleys from London. Forced by contrary winds to seek shelter, first at Shoreham and then at Plymouth and Falmouth, it was not till the 2nd of December that the convoy sailed out into the ocean. Nine days later they were at Bayona, a small seaport of Galicia, where they delayed three days, their long sea journey at length terminating on the 16th at Cascaës, whence they travelled overland to Lisbon. In the absence of the Court a letter explaining the object of the mission was entrusted to the herald Flanders, who pursued the King from Estremóz to Arrayollos and Aviz, in the province of Alemtéjo, where the embassy at last had audience of his Majesty on the 13th of January and presented to him the Duke's letters soliciting the hand of his daughter Isabella. The while the ambassadors were discussing their master's proposals with the King's Council John van Eyck was at his easel painting the Infanta's portrait, two copies of which were executed and despatched to the Court of Burgundy, one by sea and the other by land, the better to ensure safe delivery, with duplicate accounts of the mission's doings to date. The Duke's reply did not arrive until the 4th of June. A pilgrimage to Saint James of Compostella, and visits to John II., King of Castile, to the Duke of Arjona, a prince of the same royal blood, and to Mohammed, King of the City of Grenada, agreeably filled in the interval of waiting, Van Eyck naturally missing no opportunity of acquaintance with the leading painters of the day, enlarging the scope of his own observation, and no doubt leaving behind him the impress of his mastery. That the name of Van Eyck was already one to conjure with in these distant realms appears from the traditional ascription to him of a mass of painting certainly in his manner, but vastly too great to have ever been conceived by him within the limits of his stay in Portugal. Take that finest of all pictures there, the "Fons Vitae" in the board-room of the Misericordia at Oporto, and the series of twelve paintings in the Episcopal Palace at Evoca, locally claimed for Van Eyck; likewise the pictures in the church of S. Francisco at Evoca, in the round church of the Templars at Thomar, and elsewhere, which are at any rate thought there to be not unworthy of his technique, and scarcely inferior to his best masterpieces for brilliancy of colouring and beauty of portraiture. The one regrettable circumstance in relation to this visit to Portugal is that both portraits of the Infanta are to be numbered among the lost certain treasures of his art.

On their return to Lisbon in the closing days of May the embassy rejoined the Court at Cintra on the ensuing 4th by special request of the king, and the Duke of Burgundy's reply came to hand the same evening: the princess's portrait had been to the Duke's liking. All the preliminaries being now in order events sped on apace, to the signing of the marriage contract at Lisbon on the 29th of July and the solemnisation of the espousals a day later; and after a period of brilliant festivities the bridal party, to the number of some two thousand, set sail for the land of Flanders. A fortnight later four weather-beaten ships, the Infanta's of the number, lumbered into Vivero harbour in Galicia, followed later by a fifth: the remainder of the original fleet of fourteen, after battling with contrary winds, had been effectually dispersed in the subsequent storm. Again a start was made on the 6th of November, but the state of prostration to which Sir John de Lannoy had been reduced by sea-sickness compelled a further delay of over a fortnight at Ribadeu. Here the convoy was reinforced by two Florentine galleys, also bound for Flanders, and on the 25th they eventually made good their leave of Portuguese waters. The afflicted ambassador, with members of his suite, had meanwhile transferred to the Florentine galleys, a step that nearly cost them their lives, as these vessels narrowly escaped shipwreck in the vicinity of the Land's End. The other five ships put into Plymouth harbour on the 29th, but the Florentines pushed on to Sluus, where they cast anchor on the 6th of December, Sir John de Lannoy making all speed to the Duke with the glad tidings of the Infanta's safe arrival in English waters. The preparations for her reception were quickly followed by the coming of the bride, who safely accomplished her long journey's end on Christmas Day. In the midst of a carnival of popular rejoicing the union was solemnised at Bruges on the 7th of January 1430.

John van Eyck's absence had extended to slightly over fourteen months, during which, seemingly, the two portraits of the Infanta were the sole yield of his art, except we couple with them the picture known as "La belle Portugaloise" and another portrait of a Portuguese maiden of which only verbal descriptions have come down to us. In the light of all the compelling evidence of John's consummate love of Nature, amply displayed in the mass of landscape work that enriches many of his finest productions, one cannot help but be struck by the fact that he never appears to have realised the possibilities of seascape as an avenue of Art. Only in one small panel do we remember any deviation from the type of slow-running river water that he usually affected, and there we are shown small craft exposed to the mean spiteful choppiness of a wind-exposed estuary, an unconvincing picture from the utter monotony of treatment of beaten water. Is it possible that the sea in all of its countless moods failed in its appeal to the aesthetic sense of the master, with its infinite variety of elemental energy and its chaste exuberance of exquisite colouring, with all the untold modulations, moreover, in that great symphony of the ocean which stirs so deeply the soul of the true poet? Or was it that the message baffled the apprehension of the artist, and left him helpless to respond to the call? Whatever the answer—or be it that, like his leader De Lannoy, he found the sea so severe a taskmaster in the more matter-of-fact sense as to blunt the edge of his finer feelings—whatever the answer, prolific as Art had already proved through the centuries by the manifold and luscious fruits it had borne, evidently it had not yet attained to the fulness of time in which it was to bring forth its apocalypse of the sea; nor was John van Eyck its consecrate expositor.

V
PERIOD OF GREAT ENDEAVOUR

We have now reached the most important period in our painter's career, coinciding from end to end with his residence in the Flemish capital, where he died on the 9th of July 1441—a period of over ten years, in which he produced the ten dated masterpieces we are about to review, besides a large unfinished triptych and a number of other paintings to which no exact date can be affixed. Hardly had he taken up his quarters in Bruges than the Duke summoned him to Hesdin to receive instructions with regard to the work on which he was to be employed. Meanwhile, no doubt, Jodoc Vyt had secured his services for the completion of the Ghent Polyptych: probably it had been an understood thing all along that John was to finish the work at the first opportunity. From the account of his movements during the five years that had elapsed since his brother's death it is obvious that he could have spared but very brief intervals of leisure for what must, after all, have been to him a labour of love; the conclusion being that whatever proportion of the sixteen months immediately following his return from Portugal he was able to devote to the picture must stand for his share in the monumental altar-piece that at Hubert's death had already been ten years in the making.

PLATE VII.—PORTRAIT OF MARGARET VAN EYCK THE PAINTER'S WIFE

(By John van Eyck)

The daughter of the subject of Plate IV. and probably the sister of Joan Cenani in Plate V., with both of which it should be compared. In the Town Gallery, Bruges. See page 66.

In the early days of December 1431 Cardinal Albergati, special ambassador from Pope Martin V. to the Courts of France, Burgundy, and England with a view to bringing about a general peace, spent three days at the Charterhouse in Bruges as the honoured guest of the Duke, from whom Van Eyck received urgent instructions to paint the portrait that is now the property of the Imperial Gallery at Vienna. The time being all too short for the purpose, John had to be content with the exquisite drawing in silver-point on a white ground which is still preserved in the Royal Cabinet of Prints at Dresden, and which is particularly interesting because of the marginal memoranda in pencil embodying the most minute observations in the artist's own handwriting for his guidance in the execution of the painting. A remarkable portrait of a most remarkable man: for this prince of the Church, a humble son of the austere Order of the Carthusians, though raised to the Cardinalate and time after time called upon to serve the Holy See on important embassies requiring consummate prudence in regard to matters of temporal policy, discarding his family arms for a simple cross, persevered to the end in such austerities of the cloister as the wearing of a hair shirt, total abstinence from flesh-meat, and the use of bare straw for his rude pallet: a type that must have appealed to Van Eyck, for the picture is a valuable index of the painter's genius for portraiture. In or about August of the following year the Burgomasters and Town Council honoured John with a visit to his workshop, to inspect the various pictures he was then engaged on. Among these, probably, was the portrait of "Tymotheos," bearing date October 10, 1432, acquired by the National Gallery in 1857 for the modest sum of £189, 11s. (Plate III.), and the "Our Lady and Child" in the collection at Ince Hall, Ince Blundell, Liverpool, although it was not completed till 1433. The latter is a delightful instance of the singular love of domesticity which Van Eyck exemplifies with supreme confidence and success in the Arnolfini tableau, of which more anon. In the former we have a man verging on middle age, with dark complexion, blue eyes, angular features, heavy jaw, thick lips, prominent cheekbones and uplifted nose; presumably a Greek humanist and a friend of the painter, from the man's Christian name on the parapet being in Greek character and the manuscript roll he holds in his hand, and from the inscription "Léal Souvenir": by no means a handsome type, but true to nature, and presented with all the charm that Van Eyck was able to endow his least promising subjects with, the modelling being excellent, and the harmonious colouring aptly relieved by a dark background.

Somewhere about this time John's thoughts, somewhat later in life than was the custom of the age, must have been turning on matrimony on his own account, for we find him purchasing a house in the parish of Saint Giles, a quarter much affected by painters, and shortly afterwards engaged on a portrait of the man appointed to be his father-in-law; and we can picture the Duke, with whom he was ever a special favourite, being made the confidant of his intentions on the occasion of his visit to Van Eyck's workshop on the 19th of February 1433, and pleasantly encouraging him with a promise to stand sponsor for his first-born. At any rate the wedding took place, and in due course Sir Peter de Beaufremont, Lord of Chargny, held the infant at the baptismal font as proxy for Philip, whose present took the form of six silver cups weighing 12 marks, the order for payment of the account, amounting to 96l. 12s., to a local goldsmith, John Peutin, bearing date June 30, 1434; and this is the nearest approach we can get at to the date of either event. Indeed, we have no information as to the sex of the child, nor are we even acquainted with the maiden name of Van Eyck's wife, though it has been suggested, with some show of reason, that she was a sister of Joan Cenani, the wife of John Arnolfini, already referred to; and it is only within quite recent days that the painting in the National Gallery commonly spoken of as "the man with the turban" has been identified, on purely scientific lines, as the portrait of her father. If the reader will compare this likeness (Plate IV.) with that of Margaret van Eyck (Plate VII.) he must immediately be struck by the close resemblance that irresistibly suggests the relationship: the marvel is that the absolute identity of features in the two portraits escaped notice so long. The fanciful style of head-dress, except it was intended to symbolise occupation or profession, remains a puzzle; for it is difficult to conceive a man of his earnest and dignified disposition masquerading in strange attire for the mere sake of effect. The best authorities speak of him as a well-to-do merchant—specialising perhaps in Eastern wares, such as crowded the marts of the Flemish capital in the heyday of its prosperity—apparently about sixty-five years of age, the face being delicately painted in reddish-brown tones, and showing every detail with uttermost faithfulness, even to the pleats of the eyelids and at the root of the nose, and to every vein and wrinkle of the forehead. It is one of the finest exemplifications of John's rare gift of portraiture, the pleasing modesty of the artist—as revealed in the inscription "Als ich kan" (to the best of my ability)—adding, indeed, to the charm of the picture, which bears date October 21, 1433, and passed into the keeping of the National Gallery in 1851 for the sum of £315.

It is difficult to refrain from what would appear an over-use of the superlative in dealing with John van Eyck's works, but if the writer might be allowed an indulgence he would unhesitatingly avail himself of it to the full in connection with the exquisite panel (Plate V.) for the possession of which we are indebted to the honourable wounds which were the seal of Major-General Hay's part in the battle of Waterloo. After wandering about Europe as the cherished possession first of Don Diego de Guevara, councillor of Maximilian and Archduke Charles and Major-domo of Joan, Queen of Castile; next of Margaret of Austria, Governess of the Netherlands; subsequently of Mary of Hungary, and eventually of Charles III. of Spain, it fell into the acquisitive hands of the French invader of the Peninsula, and by some strange freak of fortune strayed to the apartments at Brussels in which the gallant major-general was nursed to recovery, from whose landlord he purchased it, the National Gallery in the end becoming its owner, in 1842, for the trifling sum of £730. It is the picture of a newly married couple in a homely Flemish interior, and in their attempts to solve an imaginary riddle critics have given their somewhat prolific powers of imagination an unusually free rein. For instance, the peculiar manner in which the bride sustains the gathered folds of her skirt—shown by comparison with figures of virgin saints in other of Van Eyck's paintings to have been a passing fashion of the day, if an ungraceful one—suggested to some the near approach of her lying-in, the bedstead in the background as well as the figure of St. Margaret (a favourite of women in expectation of childbirth) surmounting the back of the arm-chair naturally tending to confirm the impression; in corroboration of which the attitude of husband and wife—though the direction of look in neither lends support to the theory—is explained as a venture in chiromancy, the adept bridegroom endeavouring to read in the lines of his wife's hand the future of the coming infant: a variant elucidation representing the husband as solemnly protesting his paternity to an inexistent crowd of neighbours at the open door, seeing that the ingenious reflection of the scene in the circular convex mirror on the far wall reveals but two additional figures, probably the painter and his apprentice. Without recourse to fancy, the attitude of bridegroom and bride, hand in hand, might readily have been seen to symbolise the perfect union begot of a happy marriage. John's love of domesticity is abundantly displayed in all the detail of the work—the chandelier, with lighted taper, dependent from the ceiling, the aumbry with its couple of oranges, the cushioned bench by the window, the dainty pair of red shoes on the carpet by the bedside, the pattens of white wood with black leather latchets in the foreground, even to the dusting-brush hung on the arm-chair, and the pet griffin terrier, all helping to heighten the intimacy of the scene; while the cherry-tree in full bloom, seen through the open window against a sky of clear blue, serves to fix the season of the year in which the picture was painted. The portraits are of John Arnolfini and Joan Cenani: the former, in later years, was knighted and appointed a chamberlain at his court by Duke Philip, and from the circumstance of his burial in the chapel of the Lucchese merchants at the Austin Friars' we may presume both his nationality and calling; the latter, considered in respect of certain features, especially the eyes, eyebrows, and nose, suggests a sufficient likeness to warrant the surmise that she was a younger sister of Van Eyck's wife. The panel, which is in an almost perfect state of preservation, is a fine example of the painter's vigour of delineation and perfect blending of colour, both as regards the interior and the figures, the transparency of shadow in the flesh-tints showing the utmost delicacy of touch. The picture bears date 1434.

PLATE VIII.—THE VIRGIN AND CHILD, AND CHANCELLOR ROLIN

(By — van Eyck)

Whether the work of Hubert or of John is still in dispute: hence an interesting example for the critical student of their respective arts. Nicholas Rolin was born in 1376, was created Chancellor of Burgundy and Brabant on December 3, 1422, and died January 18, 1462. The landscape in the background is distinctly reminiscent of the scenery about Maastricht, the alma mater of the Van Eycks. The general effect of the picture is marred by an unpleasant coating of yellow varnish. Date uncertain. In the Louvre, Paris. See page 78.

About this time Van Eyck was once more in trouble with the Receiver of Flanders and his officials. Philip, adding one more to the many marks of favour reserved for his predilect painter, had bestowed on him a life-pension of 4320*l.* in lieu of the salary of 100*l.* parisis awarded him at the time of his engagement. In the absence of any explanation of this enormous increase, the mystified accountants at Lille declined registration of the letters patent; but they were speedily brought to their senses by John's threat, without further waste of words, to throw up his appointment there and then: so they referred the matter back to the Duke, who by letters of March 12, 1435, commanded immediate registration of the patent and payment of the pension under penalty of his extreme displeasure, protesting that, being about to employ Van Eyck on works of the highest importance, he "could not find another painter equally to his taste or of such excellence in his art and science." Matters being thus satisfactorily composed, John was free to attend to his patron's behests; in addition to which he had the gilding and polychroming in 1435 of six of the eight statues of counts and countesses of Flanders executed by local sculptors for the front of the new Townhouse, probably from his own designs. Yet another present of six silver cups, perhaps as a salve for his wounded feelings, and employment on a further secret mission to distant parts in 1436 testify to the Duke's abiding trust and approbation. These undertakings, however, did not exhaust the painter's marvellous capacity for work, for this year also witnessed the completion of one of the largest of his pictures, the altar-piece to the order of Canon Van der Paele, for the collegiate church of Saint Donatian at Bruges (Plate VI.), which since its recovery from the French in 1815 has graced the collection of the local Town Gallery. John's love of the Romanesque probably accounts for his neglect of the architecture of that church in designing the apse of the transept in which the Virgin and Child sit enthroned, but the scenic effect produced by his treatment of the series of round arches on cylindrical columns and of the pillared ambulatory goes far to compensate for the omission; the beauty of the picture being further enhanced by the ornate carving of the capitals and throne, the gorgeous display of cloth-of-gold and tapestry, and the rich variety of dress and costume, culminating in all the splendour of the archiepiscopal vestments, yet not so overpowering as to dwarf interest in the noble countenance of the wearer. Howbeit, the artist was singularly unfortunate in the subjects appointed to pose for the Virgin and St. George, while the Divine Child is probably the least pleasing of his Infant Christs. St. Donatian, however, and the homely yet dignified ecclesiastic typified as the Donor, largely redeem the figure-work from the charge of insignificance. It would appear that the life-size bust of Canon Van der Paele at Hampton Court Palace was a study for the full-length portrait, for at the time the altar-piece was being executed the worthy Canon was already so feeble that since September 1434 he had been dispensed by the Chapter from attendance in choir on the score of infirmity and advanced age.

The "Portrait of John De Leeuw, goldsmith," in the Imperial Gallery at Vienna (1436), and two charming pictures in the Antwerp Museum—"Saint Barbara" (1437) and the "Our Lady and Child by a Fountain" (1439)—come next in order of the artist's dated pieces, the series closing with the "Portrait of Margaret van Eyck" (Plate VII.) in the Town Gallery at Bruges, which bears date June 17, 1439: a work of marvellous delicacy and finish, and a tribute of love worthy alike of the painter-husband and his devoted wife; the latter an intelligent type of the competent Flemish housewife, clear and steady of eye and firm of mouth, portrayed with infinite minuteness and not the least concession to vanity. Formerly the property of the Guild of Painters and Saddlers, it used annually to be exhibited in their chapel on St. Luke's Day, amply secured, if we believe the popular legend, with chain and padlock, because of the companion picture, Van Eyck's own portrait, having been stolen through lack of similar precautions.

The sad loss to Art sustained by John van Eyck's death on the 9th of July 1441 is accentuated by the unfinished state in which he left the great triptych on which he was engaged for Nicholas van Maelbeke, Provost of Saint Martin's at Ypres, his largest painting and, had he but lived to complete it, in every respect his masterpiece. As a member of the Duke's household John was buried within the precincts of the collegiate church of St. Donatian, and his remains finally laid to rest some months later within the building, near the font; and an anniversary Requiem Mass, founded at the time, continued to be celebrated until the French invasion in 1792. In death as in life Duke Philip never forgot his faithful friend and servant: within a few days of his decease he sought to solace the widow's grief with a gratuity of 360*l.* in token of his appreciation of the great master whose death they all mourned, and years after he graciously assisted Livina, the one surviving child of the marriage, and a sister of his own godchild, to enter the Convent of St. Agnes at Maaseyck.

A NOTE IN CONCLUSION

However representative the great masterpieces which it has been possible to notice within the scope of this monograph, we are far yet from having covered the art of the Van Eycks; and, strangely enough, the same difficulty that is met in apportioning to each his share in the Great Polyptych recurs when seeking to ascribe a number of other paintings which are certainly the work of one or other of the brothers. The study of these will always appeal to the intelligent student of their art, and as a typical example of the group we present the altar-piece known as "The Blessed Virgin and Child and Chancellor Rolin" (Plate VIII.), in the Louvre, Paris: a remarkable work in respect of types, of portraiture, and of landscape, every detail of which has been elaborated to a degree scarcely conceivable. Many other of their paintings are to be found scattered over Europe, along with much that is the work of copyist, pupil, or imitator, too often with idle claims to authenticity; for the influence of the Van Eycks was coextensive with the art world of their day. Truthfulness, it has been observed, was the dominant note of their art, and by their sedulous cultivation of Truth they dominated the art of their age. With John this love of truth amounted well-nigh to a passion; and the reproach of the carping critic to whom beauty of feature alone makes for beauty of portraiture fails of its effect on the true artist mind, to whom the faithful record of all trifling blemishes of the face is but an added testimony and guarantee of the fidelity of the portrait as a portrait of the inner as well as of the outer man. Even a great painter may enhance his present popularity and widen his clientèle by a flattering suppression of personal disfigurement, but only to the injury of his fame and the hurt of his own self-respect. John van Eyck scorned to grovel at the feet of Vanity, and with this acknowledgment of the sense and honesty of his sitters he combined the fulfilment of a duty to posterity, for with the true instinct of genius he knew that he was painting not for his own brief day, but for all time, and that, as the founder of a great school of portraiture and the father of landscape art, it behoved him to set an example of the cardinal principle which should direct them. Under any conditions John van Eyck's genius must have asserted itself, but happily it was fortunate in its setting, for the brilliancy of the great Burgundian court and the sumptuous patronage of Duke Philip in the full blaze of his power and glory were invaluable aids to the production and dissemination of his art. Nor did success spoil his sterling nature: amidst all the triumphs of his life his character remained singularly free from the tarnish of empty pride, to the last the exquisite yield of his art being given to the world in a charming spirit of apology so aptly embodied in the simple motto of his choosing, "Als ich kan." And who among all the great painters of the after ages has done better?

Milton Keynes UK
Ingram Content Group UK Ltd.
UKHW030744071024
449371UK00006B/577

9 789362 923035